DON'T EVER LOOK BEHIND DOOR 32

Don't Ever Look Behind Door 32

B.C.R. Fegan

All rights reserved. No part of this publication may be reproduced, copied or transmitted without prior permission of the author.

Copyright © B.C.R. Fegan 2017

Cover art and illustrations by L. Wen

The moral right of the author has been asserted.

Published by TaleBlade Press

TaleBlade

www.taleblade.com

For Jackson.

DON'T EVER LOOK BEHIND DOOR 32

B.C.R. FEGAN

ILLUSTRATED BY
LENNY WEN

TaleBlade

Welcome to the magical Hotel of Hoo,

Where I'll be your host, Mr Nicholas Noo.

I'm sure you'll be happy in room number 1.

You'll be my first guests; before you, I had none.

Please explore my hotel, but whatever you do,

Don't ever look behind door 32.

Through door number 2 are the grumpy old clowns.
I don't think they're funny,
but they help clean the grounds.

Through door number 3 are the fidgety knights.
They itch and they scratch,
but they fix all the lights.

Through door number 4 is the room where we eat.

Whenever you're hungry, come in, take a seat.

But just a reminder, when done with your stew,

Don't ever look behind door 32.

Through door number 5 are the zombies who dance.

They'll mend all your shirts and help fix your pants.

Through door number 6 is nothing at all:

Not a roof, not a floor, not even a wall.

You'll find purple goblins through door number 8.
The zombies don't like them,
but I think they're great.

A mysterious box is in room number 10.
One day it appeared: I can't recall when.
If you know what is in it, please give me a clue.
Just don't ever look behind door 32.

Number 11, it isn't a room
But a cupboard of mops and a tiny red broom.

Through door number 12 are unusual pets.
A few are quite ill, but the goblins are vets.

There are miniature giants in number 13.
They all seem like us; you'll see what I mean.
And while you both wonder why none of them grew,
Don't even contemplate door 32.

The vampire mermaids in number 14.
They pick up the trash and keep the pool clean.

In number 15 I keep all my trees.
I'd keep them outside but they don't like the breeze.

In number 16 is the bathroom of gold.

The toilets look great but the seats are quite cold.

And if in the morning you find there's a queue,

Don't go and seek out door 32.

There's tea-loving monsters through door 17
With manners the best that I've ever seen.

Room 18 has the scariest ghosts.
They help in the kitchen and cook all the roasts.

Through door number 20 are cute little elves.

They help in the library and sleep on the shelves.

You'll see wingless dragons through door 21.

Unable to fly but still lots of fun.

Another guest room is through door 22.

Did you really think that just one would do?

And I'd tell all guests the same I told you,

Don't ever look behind door 32.

I keep evil fairies in room 23.

They cause quite a mess but I got them for free.

There's big-headed monkeys in room 24.
They dust all the walls and help sweep the floor.

Room 25 is where I keep my treasure.
You're welcome to look anytime at your pleasure.
And please, as a gift, take a jewel when you're through.
Just don't ever look behind door 32.

You'll find baby wizards in room 26.
Just ask them politely: they'll show you some tricks.

But you will find nothing on room 32.

In room number 30 are very old trolls.

Before they moved in, they were living in holes.

Room 31 is a very dark place.

You won't see your hand in front of your face.

In fact, I don't think any light can get through

In that strange unlit room beside door 32.

And so I suppose as you take in the view

And wander the halls and meet all the crew,

You'll find yourselves standing at door 32,

And both of you'll wonder, "What if we went through?

Why shouldn't we look behind door 32?"

Well, I'll tell you. You see, it's not what's there, but who . . .

It's in fact where I live,
Mr Nicholas Noo.

And I just want my privacy
here – wouldn't you?

CPSIA information can be obtained
at www.ICGtesting.com
Printed in the USA
LVHW01n0217130218
566349LV00008B/13/P